D0655546

COUNTY LIBRARY

WITHDRAWN FROM STOCK

THE ESSENTIAL
GABRIEL FITZMAURICE

PRAISE FOR GABRIEL FITZMAURICE

'[T]he best contemporary, traditional, popular poet in English.'

Ray Olson, *Booklist* (US)

'Fitzmaurice is a wonderful poet.'

Giles Foden, *The Guardian* (UK)

'He has a gift for making the quotidian interesting and investing the ordinary with extraordinary significance.'

Gearóid Mac Lochlainn, *The Celtic Pen*

'[Fitzmaurice] is poetry's answer to J[ohn] B. Keane.'

Fred Johnston, *Books Ireland*

THE ESSENTIAL
GABRIEL FITZMAURICE

Selected Poems & Translations

821/FIT.

Illustrated
by
BRENDA FITZMAURICE

MERCIER PRESS
WHAT YOU NEED TO READ

Mercier Press
Cork
www.mercierpress.ie

Trade enquiries to:
CMD Distribution,
55A Spruce Avenue, Stillorgan Industrial Park,
Blackrock, Co. Dublin.

© Text, Gabriel Fitzmaurice, 2008
© Illustrations, including cover illustration, Brenda
Fitzmaurice, 2008

A CIP record for this title is available from the British Library

ISBN: 978 1 85635 592 6

10 9 8 7 6 5 4 3 2 1

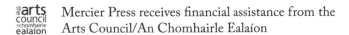 Mercier Press receives financial assistance from the
Arts Council/An Chomhairle Ealaíon

This book is sold subject to the condition that it shall not, by way of trade or
otherwise, be lent, resold, hired out or otherwise circulated without the pub-
lisher's prior consent in any form of binding or cover other than that in which
it is published and without a similar condition including this condition being
imposed on the subsequent purchaser.

No part of this publication may be reproduced or transmitted in any form or by
any means, electronic or mechanical, including photocopying, recording or any
information or retrieval system, without the prior permission of the publisher
in writing.

Printed and bound in the EU

In memory of my father and mother,
Jack and Maud Fitzmaurice,
and especially for Brenda, John and Nessa,
with love

CONTENTS

Acknowledgements	11
Preface	13
Introduction *by Fintan O'Toole*	17

From *Rainsong* (1984)

Portaireacht Bhéil	27
Derelicts	28
Stale Porter	30
Reading Kinsella in the *Brasserie*	31
Garden	33

From *Road to the Horizon* (1987)

A Game of Forty-one	34
Parting	37
Stripping a Chair	38
The Hurt Bird	40
The Poet's Garden	47

From *Dancing Through* (1990)

In the Midst of Possibility	48
Getting to Know You	49

From *The Village Sings* (1996)

Galvin and Vicars	51

The Village Hall 53

At the Ball Game 55

Fireplace 56

Mary 57

'I Thirst' 58

Good Friday 60

In Memoriam Danny Cunningham 1912–1995 61

May Dalton 62

From *A Wrenboy's Carnival* (2000)

Sonnet to Brenda 63

Gaeltacht 64

Dan Breen 65

Knocklong 66

A Parent's Love 68

Listening to *Desperados Waiting for a Train* 70

Ode to a Pint of Guinness 71

The Woman of the House 73

Dad 77

In Memory of my Mother 78

So what if there's no Happy Ending? 79

Requiescat 80

In the Woods 82

From *I and the Village* (2002)

To my D–28 83

The *Díseart* 85

Country Life   87
On Declining a Commission   88
Scorn not the Ballad   89
Alzheimer's Disease   90
Lassie   91
Knockanure Church   92

From *Poems from the Irish* (2004)
The Yellow Bittern   94
Cill Aodáin   96
Dónall Óg   97
The Bog-deal Board   100
Brown Eyes   102
A Change   104
Christmas Eve   105
Vietnam Love Song   106
Captivity   108
The Purge   109
Here at *Caiseal na gCorr* Station   125
A Braddy Cow   127
To Jack Kerouac   129
My Blackhaired Love   132

From *The Boghole Boys* (2005)
The Celebrant's a Critic   133
The Ballad of Rudi Doody   134
Mairg Nach Fuil 'na Dhubhthuata   137

A Local Murder 138

The Day Christ Came to Moyvane 139

Before the Word 'Fuck' Came
  to Common Use 140

The Mission Magazines 142

On Hearing Johnny Cash's
  American Recordings 143

His Last Pint 144

The Mother 145

Munster Football Final 1924 146

A Footballer 147

Poem for Nessa, Five Years Old 148

Poem for John 149

A Widower 150

Home 151

The Fitzs Come to Town 152

For the Fitzmaurices of Glenalappa 153

From *Twenty-one Sonnets* (2007)

On First Meeting the Marquess
  of Lansdowne 156

True Love 157

Homage to Thomas MacGreevy 158

A Middle Aged Orpheus Looks
  back at his Life 159

ACKNOWLEDGEMENTS

I am indebted to the editors and publishers who first published the poems in this collection which I've taken from the following publications: *Rainsong* (Beaver Row Press, Dublin, 1984), *Road to the Horizon* (Beaver Row Press, 1987), *Dancing Through* (Beaver Row Press, 1990), *The Village Sings* (Story Line Press, Oregon, Cló Iar-Chonnachta, Conamara, Peterloo Poets, Cornwall, 1996), *A Wrenboy's Carnival* (Wolfhound Press, Dublin, Peterloo Poets, 2000), *I and the Village* (Marino Books, Dublin, 2002), *The Boghole Boys* (Marino Books, Cork, 2005) and *Twenty-one Sonnets* (Salmon Poetry, Cliffs of Moher, 2007).

I would like to thank the following for permission to include my translations: Caoimhín Ó Marcaigh for Seán Ó Riordáin's poems; Máire Mhac an tSaoi; Cathal Ó Luain for Caitlín Maude's poems; The Gallery Press and the estate of Michael Hartnett for Michael Hartnett's poem; Cló Iar-Chonnachta for Cathal Ó Searcaigh's poems.

Preface

Why this book? Well, to begin with, I believe it contains the poems of mine that work best on the page and on the stage. The page and stage have always been important to me. How many times do we hear good poems done to death by bad presentation at poetry readings? And how many bad poems are mutton dressed as lamb when they are well recited?

I have always wanted to be a popular poet. But a serious one. As far back as I can remember, I have wanted to write poetry. And a significant part of the poetry I admire is song. Poets like Kris Kristofferson and Leonard Cohen have set their words to music. They are giants at my shoulder. I set myself the task of making my words sing without the benefit of a musical score.

The Essential Gabriel Fitzmaurice, a title I've stolen from the musical world, contains, literally, my greatest hits – the poems people buy, the poems people request at my readings, the ones, even, that people recite in pubs, at parties, at musical evenings. As the books in which these poems were first published are now out of print, and as people keep wanting to buy these poems, Mercier Press and I decided to make them available again.

I have included poems from my adult collections and from my translations from the Irish. I have not included any of my poems for children as a selection of them will make another volume at some time in the future. In any case, it's best, I feel, to keep them separate. When I write for children, I enter a child's mind; when I write for adults, I get to know my own.

Poetry, for me, has always been my way of saying myself, of making sense of my world. This has, inevitably, meant that I write out of my environment, physical, emotional and spiritual. To date, many critics have concentrated on my physical environment, my home place, in their readings of my work. But the emotional and spiritual are eclipsed in this interpretation. And this, I feel, is a mistake.

So here is *The Essential Gabriel Fitzmaurice*. I offer it to the reader as a loving, honest celebration. But the celebrant is also a critic. A constructive critic. A sympathetic critic. There is no point in hollow celebration or in empty praise. I do not turn a blind eye to ugliness in my environment. But I refuse to wallow in it. As I have written elsewhere, 'When art distorts the truth, it is obscene'. There are enough writers willing to distort the truth without my adding to their number.

In the final analysis, this is where I come from, this is where I write out of. I offer it in humility to you, dear reader. I hope you will profit from the reading. And enjoy.

GABRIEL FITZMAURICE

INTRODUCTION

When the architectural historian Deyan Sudjic was going through the files of the Dublin-based architects Scott Tallon Walker, he was especially struck by one photograph in particular. It showed a group of male parishioners streaming out of Knockanure church near Gabriel Fitzmaurice's native village of Moyvane, Co. Kerry. It was taken shortly after the chapel was built in 1964. The church, designed by Michael Scott, is an austere, defiantly unadorned modernist box, with sharp angles, a box-like shape and, instead of a steeple, a concrete roof floating above a transparent glass wall that seems too fragile to support it. But the faces of the men, wearing their flat caps and Sunday best, struck Sudjic as if they could be from the 1930s or even the 1890s. The conjunction of the two images, one redolent of change and strangeness, the other of continuity and familiarity, was much more true to the place than either one on its own could ever have been.

That church is at the centre of one of Gabriel Fitzmaurice's defining poems, 'Knockanure Church'. In it, he begins by noting its 'out of date' 1960s modernism and its deep unpopularity as the 'garage on the hill' that replaced a much-loved traditional chapel. The poem itself is a variant of the traditional Shakespearian sonnet and its familiar patterns and insistent rhymes seem to place it on the side of the disgruntled parishioners, pining for a more familiar past. For the first six lines, it seems to affirm a lazy perception of Gabriel Fitzmaurice as primarily a poet of an old, rural and all but vanished Ireland.

Yet a good sonnet contains and explores tensions and ambiguities, and its energy is all in its twist, the turn that shifts the weight from one idea to another. The turn here is the poet's complete identification with the building that 'local people seem to hate'. He offers 'Knockanure Church' to us as a kind of self-portrait in concrete and glass:

> My God's a God who strips me in this place –
> No cover here, the lines are stark and spare;
> Through the years, I've grown into this space ...

The poem – and by extension the poet – are thus akin to that photograph that struck Dejan Sudjic so powerfully. Fitzmaurice is sufficiently of the 'local people' to understand, and to a degree articulate, their feelings about the church. He is also sufficiently outside them to be able to use a phrase like 'local people' in a way that makes clear his own exclusion from that collective identity. He belongs in some sense with the men in the photograph, in their flat caps and Sunday best, who could be living in the 1930s. But he belongs even more in the lonely, uncovered space of rigorous lines and sharp angles: the space of art and of faith. The importance of this pared-back, ruthlessly-culled, collection of his work is that it strips away those elements of his achievement that can make him appear, misleadingly, the bard of Moyvane. All the clarity and approachability that make him so rightly popular have been preserved, but the toughness, the tension and the restlessness of 'lines [that] are stark and spare' is much more apparent. Like Johnny Cash's *American Recordings*, that are so powerfully evoked here, his impulse is to seek truth in what remains when everything superfluous has been dispensed with: 'To pare life back to where things don't deceive'.

That essence is spiritual, rather than social. If there is an over-arching theme in this collection, it is the emergence of, in the very broadest sense, a religious poet. It is not accidental that the two sides of Fitzmaurice's vision are best appreciated by reading 'Knockanure Church' alongside another poem set in a church, the brilliantly wrought 'I Thirst'. The two poems show the range of Fitzmaurice's mastery of traditional forms – the sonnet on the one side and the ballad on the other. 'I Thirst', with its driving narrative and apparently simple rhymes, also starts with what seems an easy evocation of communal tradition – Midnight Mass on Christmas Eve. As in 'Knockanure Church', this sense of common values is disrupted by an outside force – in this case the drunk who has gone from the pub to the church, carrying two bottles of stout. His gesture at the offertory of leaving the bottles of stout on the altar rails turns the solemnities into an 'unholy farce'. But the poet turns it back to the sacred, evoking the Christ on the Cross, whose virtual last words were the simple human cry 'I thirst'. Those words became the motto of the great Catholic mystic, Therese of Lisieux.

Within a deceptively simple form, therefore, Fitzmaurice embraces the profane and the sacred, unholy farce and mystical vision, social comedy and a rough but profound spirituality. And this range is typical. The ballast of 'I Thirst' may be provided by a lusty, Rabelaisian, almost mediaeval energy, but the wind in its sails is a quiet, surprisingly tender devotion. Conversely, the weight of 'Knockanure Church' lies on the side of a lonely, almost aloof, devotion, but it evokes the communal and the mundane with respect and understanding. Together, the poems remind us that, in art, nothing is quite so complicated as simplicity.

It is easy to categorise Fitzmaurice as a rural poet, for instance, and he himself imagines the possible viewpoint of those who might read him as a vestige of a lost world:

> ... scholars will read it to get one last look
> At the village before it has lost its own story
>
> ('Ode to a Pint of Guinness')

The rustic image is plausible enough until you notice the absence in these poems of any romantic evocations of nature or of the lexicon of an agricultural childhood that we associate most obviously with Seamus Heaney. In fact, Fitzmaurice is as much an urban poet as a rural one. When he evokes Moyvane, he tends to call it a town. He is a laureate of the Great Indoors. Most of these poems develop within four walls, in churches, pubs, the classroom, the village hall, the home.

Nature is evoked, not through wild landscape or creatures, but through that most civilised of spaces, the garden. What's cultivated there is not nature, but love and literature. In the poem of that name, the garden serves as a ground watered by love and (through the poem's incantatory rhythm and the delicately-placed image of viaticum, the eucharist of the dying) prayer. In 'The Poet's Garden', the metaphor of the garden begins as an apparently conventional image of bees and flowers but unfolds into a wry and elegant description of the pleasures and torments of literary life. Likewise, when a bird forms the centre of a poem, as it does in the deftly controlled drama of 'The Hurt Bird', it comes in to illuminate, not nature, but humanity: the clear, transforming vision of childhood.

It is true, of course, that Fitzmaurice's habitual terrain is defined by the old landmarks and milestones of Catholic and nationalist Ireland: family, church, home, the GAA, the Irish language, the War of Independence. He is probably more in touch with the common currency of Irish culture than any other writer. But precisely because he is so close to it, he can view it, not just without malice, but also without romance or nostalgia. Here again, what marks his poetic exploration of this world is tension. He writes, accurately and with a hint of defiance, that 'Some things don't go away/ Easily' ('Galvin and Vicars') but he is bullet-proof against nostalgia. In 'Before the Word "Fuck" Came to Common Use', he demolishes with a cold, controlled anger, the oft-heard complaint that Ireland has become a coarser society:

> Before the word 'fuck' came to common use
> Children mattered less than their abusers.

Piety of any sort is utterly alien to him. Fitzmaurice's love for the Irish language is expressed here, not by chance, in vibrant, vigorous translations of both classical and contemporary poets that give expression to a sense of that tradition, not just as a living thing, but as an urgent, demotic, complicated engagement with life. His deep connection to Catholicism does not make him any less clear-eyed about the tyranny it once exerted. In the carefully balanced gentleness and rage of 'Alzheimer's Disease', he notes 'How the good are frightened of their Church' and probes the persistence of fear, even in a woman who has forgotten everything else: 'the past is as today/Where she was damned unless she would obey.' His loyalty to his village does not stop him, in 'A Game of Forty-one' wishing there were some:

> Other way of spending
> A lifetime in this town.

His intense sense of place is matched by an acute sense of displacement. He is too honest and unblinking to pretend that the community he loves is some kind of organic whole, for he knows that its wholeness has long been rent asunder by emigration. Fitzmaurice is sometimes reminiscent of the playwright Tom Murphy in his description of the strange psychology of exile. He sees the returned exiles in the country pubs, watches, in 'The Ballad of Rudi Doody', 'Home' and 'The Fitzs Come to Town':

> The ones who, returning to Moyvane,
> Brought England with them in the way they dressed.

or, as in 'The Woman of the House', are:

> ... out to prove that exile
> Does better than the rest ...

The raw admiration for the fierce courage that won the War of Independence that is captured in 'The Mother' is tempered by the ambivalence of 'Dan Breen' and by the imaginative reconciliation in 'Galvin and Vicars', which mourns together two men shot within a week of each other in the Moyvane area, the republican Mick Galvin and the old scion of the ascendancy, Sir Arthur Vicars. The immensely tender conjuring of family ties in poems like 'Dad' and 'In Memory of My Mother' is complicated both by the sadness of his mother's illness and early death, and by the consequent quiet subversion of gender roles:

> A man before his time, he cooked and sewed,
> Took care of me – and Mammy in her bed ...

Indeed, of all the great markers of traditional Ireland, the only one that Fitzmaurice leaves untouched is the GAA. He is a Kerryman after all, and never more so than in his ability to pay homage to Gaelic football, in poems like 'A Footballer', 'Munster Football Final 1924' and 'At the Ball Game', as the crucible of truth, of poetry and of virtue. In Kerry, at least one thing is still worthy of unalloyed reverence.

Yet that sharpness of vision, and the tension that gives these poems their energy, does not stop Fitzmaurice's work from having the directness, and often the delight, of music. Ezra Pound wrote that 'music begins to atrophy when it departs too far from the dance; [and] that poetry begins to atrophy when it gets too far from music.' It is no accident, surely, that this collection begins and ends with music, starting with the subtle distillation of the marriage of poetry and music in *Portaireacht Bhéil* and ending with the witty and rueful evocation of mortality through music in 'A Middle-aged Orpheus Looks Back at His Life'. In between, Fitzmaurice honours Pound's injunction and never gets too far from music. Here too the points of reference are eclectic, as the landmarks are set both in the distant past and the contemporary world. From 'Desperados Waiting for a Train' to 'The Yellow Bittern' and from 'Donal Óg' to Johnny Cash's *American Recordings,* the soundtrack of this collection is multi-layered. But the underlying note is constant. It is the sense that what is played is ultimately not the music, but the self that is seeking expression in the people and things around it. Reading these poems, I thought of Walt Whitman's old lines:

> All music is what awakes from you when you
> are reminded by the instruments ...

The instruments here are words formed under the pressure of an unending search for the essence of things.

FINTAN O'TOOLE

PORTAIREACHT BHÉIL

Who would make music hears in himself
The tune that he must play.
He lilts the inarticulate.
He wills cacophony obey.

Portaireacht Bhéil: (Irish) mouth music, lilting, humming

DERELICTS

Whenever I picture the village fools
They drool with the hump
Of benevolence on their backs.
Living in hovels as I remember,
They had the health of the rat.

They perched on the street-corner
Like crows around the carcass
Of a lamb. Stale bread and sausages
Would feed a hungry man.
Beady with the cunning of survival,
Each pecked the other from his carrion.

Children feared them like rats in a sewer –
They stoned their cabins
And the stones lay at the door.

Like priests, they were the expected,
The necessary contrary –
We bow in gratitude for mediocre lives;
We keep the crow, the rat from the garden.
Like priests, no one mourned when they died.

When they died, we pulled down their cabins;
Then we transported a lawn
That the mad, the hopeless might be buried –
Only the strong resisting (while strong).
We kept the grass and flower-beds neatly
But the wilderness wouldn't be put down.

Children no longer play there
(They stone it),
Nettles stalk the wild grass,
Scutch binds the stones together ...

Then came the rats.

STALE PORTER

'Love is too big for people,
They only live together in the end',
I wrote, a lovesick adolescent.

Now a paunchy thirty
With marriage willowing in porter,
Velvet, lily cream,
I wonder.

She was velvet, lily cream,
And then I loved her
And love her yet
Through froth of hate:

We ate the prawns of love.

So once again your love you banished
Leaving you alone.
Leash your gun-dog for a walk
And pick up the telephone.

READING KINSELLA IN THE *BRASSERIE*
WHILE THE WIFE IS DOING HER HAIR

What am I doing here
Reading Kinsella in the *Brasserie*
While the wife is doing her hair?

Later I'll mosey to Montmartre
And join the poets in Place du Tertre;
And then maybe I'll go to Chartres
And take a photo of the glass
(Will I say a prayer?)
I'm reading Kinsella in the *Brasserie*
While the wife is doing her hair.

I turn the pages absently
Reading Kinsella in the *Brasserie*
In my head a dream of whores –
I ravish them, they ravish me
Reading Kinsella in the *Brasserie*
While the wife is doing her hair.

And every day I sip cold beer
Turning pages sitting here
Framed again in the window pane
While the wife is doing her hair.

The *serveuse*, smiling, seems to say to me
'Why are you alone in the *Brasserie?*'
Oh, I'd tell her I don't care.
I'd buy her a beer or a Burgundy
And I wouldn't be alone in the *Brasserie*
(Perhaps we'd go upstairs)

But I'm reading Kinsella in the *Brasserie*
While the wife is doing her hair.

GARDEN

For Brenda

We were a garden dug by eager hands;
Weeds were swept by shovels underground;
Brown earth, blackened and split by winter,
Was picked to a skeleton by starving birds.

Spring surprised us with a yelp of daisies
Defiant as a terrier guarding his home ground;
We planted seed in the cleft of drills
Slimy with earthworms.

Today I picked the first fruit of our garden –
Bloody with earth, I offered it to you;
You washed it and anointed it,
We ate it like viaticum.

In the eating of pith and seed
I loved you.

A GAME OF FORTY-ONE

Tonight it's forty-one:
Pay to your right, 10p a man.
Doubles a jink, and play your hand.
If you renege, we'll turn you.

Yes, tonight it's forty-one:
A table for six, any pub in town.
Follow suit, and stand your round.
If you renege, we'll turn you.

Tonight it's forty-one
And tomorrow in the Dáil
Fine Gael and Fianna Fáil
Debate their Bill –

'Cos on the television
They're talking of revision
And extension of detention
And extra Special Powers.

So we sit here hour by hour
Getting drunk on special Power:
A game of cards at night now
Costs more and more and more.

And you trump hard on the table,
And you pay up when you're able.
If you don't, then you're in trouble –
It's worse than to renege.

Oh, it's always forty-one:
Play your cards at work, at home –
Even sitting on a barstool
They won't let you alone.

Yes, it's always forty-one,
And I'm really in the dumps
For the horsemouth at my elbow
Has just led the ace of trumps.

And I'm playing forty-one
And wishing there were some
Other way of spending
A lifetime in this town.

But the poet and the priest
– Beauty and the Beast –
Must all sit down together
And cut this common deck.

And there is no bill or bible
But the verdict of the table
And the argument of players
To dispute the point of rule.

So tonight it's forty-one
And tomorrow, next week, next month,
And I'm out if I suggest
Another rule.

We'll turn you: (dialect) We'll put you out of this round of cards
The Dáil: (Irish) The parliament of the Irish Republic
Fine Gael and Fianna Fáil: The two largest political parties in
the Irish Republic

PARTING

Past is past
And loving ends,
And meeting thus,
We're old friends.

As loving ends
When past is past,
Here at her funeral
We are friends at last.

And the coffin slips
Through the church door
Like the love of lovers
Who were nothing more.

For past is past
And love is changed
And behind her coffin
We speak again.

With the shovels parting
The black earth for her,
We part again
This living squalor.

STRIPPING A CHAIR

For Desmond Egan

Gloss dissolves
Then wrinkles.

Layers peel
To the first bonding
Of paint and wood.

The knife cuts
Through generations
Of enhancement

Till further stripping
Damages the wood.

Grit reaches
To the residue
Of the first painting

As the first crude vision
Is sanded smooth.

This was the true vision.
Who made this chair was no craftsman
Of curve and mortise –

This chair served its purpose
And didn't interrupt
The daily drudge.

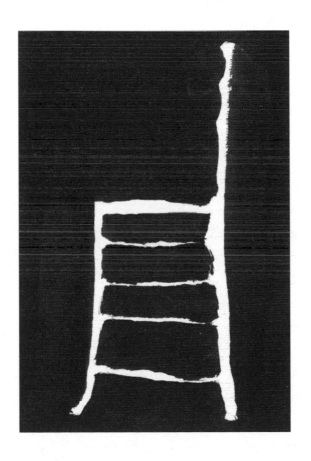

THE HURT BIRD

After playtime
Huddled in the classroom ...

In the yard
Jackdaws peck the ice
While the class guesses
The black birds:

Blackbirds?
(Laughter).

Crows?
Well yes ...
But jackdaws.
Those are jackdaws.
Why do they peck the ice?

Wonder
Becomes jackdaws' eyes
Rummaging the ice

Till suddenly
At the window opposite
– Oh the bird!

The poor bird!
At the shout
The jackdaws fright.

Sir, a robin sir ...
He struck the window
And he fell
And now he's dying
With his legs up
On the ice:

The jackdaws
Will attack it sir,

They will rip its puddings out.

I take the wounded bird,
Deadweight
In my open palm

– No flutter
No escaping

And lay it on the floor near heat,
The deadweight
Of the wound
Upon my coat.

Grasping
The ways of pain,
The pain of birds
They cannot name,
The class are curious
But quiet:

They will not frighten
The struggle
Of death and living.

Please sir,
Will he die?

And I
Cannot reply.

Alone
With utter pain

Eyes closed

The little body
Puffed and gasping
Lopsided
Yet upright:

He's alive,
The children whisper
Excited
As if witnessing
His birth.

Would he drink water sir?
Would he eat bread?
Should we feed him?

Lopsided
The hurt bird
With one eye open
To the world
Shits;

He moves
And stumbles

I move
To the hurt bird:
The beak opens
– For food
Or fight?

I touch
The puffed red breast

With trepid finger;
I spoon water
To the throat:

It splutters.

Children crumb their lunches
Pleading to lay the broken bread
Within reach of the black head.

The bird
Too hurt to feed
Falls in the valley
Of the coat,
And as I help
It claws
And perches on my finger
Bridging the great divide
Of man and bird.

He hops
From my finger
To the floor

And flutters
Under tables
Under chairs

Till exhausted
He tucks his head
Between wing and breast
Private
Between coat and wall.
The class
Delights in silence
At the sleeping bird.

The bird sir ...
What is it –
A robin?
– Look at the red breast.
But you never see a robin
With a black head.

I tell them
It's a bullfinch
Explaining the colours why.

I answer their questions
From the library.
And the children draw the bullfinch
– With hurt
And gasp
And life
With the fearlessness of pain

Where the bird will fright

And in the children's pictures
Even black and grey
Are bright.

THE POET'S GARDEN

There's a pollen of bees
In the heart of the flowers

A survival of grubs
In the cabbage

A compost of words
At one end of the plot

At the other
A stillbirth of garbage.

IN THE MIDST OF POSSIBILITY

Now I love you
Free of me:
In this loving I can see
The *You* of you
Apart from me –
The *You* of you that's ever free.

This is the *You* I love.
This is the *You* I'll never have.
This is the *You* beyond possession –

The *You* that's ever true
While ever changing,
Ever new.

Now,
Naked,
Free,
The *You* of you
Meets the *Me* of me
And to see is to love,
To love, to see:

In the midst of possibility
We agree.

GETTING TO KNOW YOU

Thomas,
You don't trust me –
I can tell from your trapped eyes.
How can I help you,
My sulky friend?
Tell you I love you?
(That would seem like lies).
To reach out to touch you
Might offend.

Give you your head;
Watch over
In so far as any human can;
Coax you with tacit kindness;
Greet you, man to man ...

Yes, Thomas,
I am strong
(But equal) –
And, Thomas,
We are both 'at school':
Both circling round
A common understanding,
Both sniffing at the smile

That sweetens rules.

Today you bounce up to me,
Your eyes the rising sun:

We share your secret story –

Hello!
God bless you,
Tom ...

GALVIN AND VICARS

In memoriam Mick Galvin, killed in action, Kilmorna, Knocka-
nure (in the parish of Newtown Sandes, now Moyvane) on
Thursday, 7 April, 1921; *Sir Arthur Vicars,* shot at Kilmorna
House, his residence, on Thursday, 14 April 1921.

Mick Galvin, Republican,
Arthur Vicars, who knows what?
– Some sort of loyalist –
In Ireland's name were shot:

Vicars by republicans,
Galvin by the *Tans,*
Both part of my history
The parish of Newtown Sandes

Named to flatter landlords
(But 'Moyvane' today,
Though some still call it 'Newtown' –
Some things don't go away

Easily). Galvin and Vicars,
I imagine you as one –
Obverse and reverse
Sundered by the gun.

History demands
We admit each other's wrongs:
Galvin and Vicars,
Joined only in this song,

Nonetheless I join you
In the freedom of this state
For art discovers symmetries
Where politics must wait.

Tans: i.e. *Black and Tans,* a unit of the crown forces during the
Irish War of Independence

THE VILLAGE HALL

The old hall with its shaky stage
Was good enough for us –
Bill Horan and Eileen Manaher
Wholly marvellous

As they called up here before us
A world of their own,
The magic I have grown to love,
The farce I loved, outgrown.

The queue outside the musty hall,
The key turned in the lock,
The stampede to the benches,
The fizz, the sweets, clove rock;

And then the silence as the play
Took us in its spell,
Local folk turned gods and queens
In this miracle.

The hall is old, not worth repair,
They'll knock it, build anew;
My boy and girl will taste in there
The magic that I knew;

They'll find the things a village finds
In the local hall –
That as Eileen becomes a queen
We're not ourselves at all.

AT THE BALL GAME

For Seamus Heaney

Everything out there you see
Is a version of reality
As heroes triumph over doubt
And bring their kind of truth about.

Each, according to his way,
Engages on the field of play,
And, urging on, the faithful crowd
Are cheering, praising, cursing loud
For beauty only will suffice,
Beauty to infuse our lives:
No cup, no trophy will redeem
Victory by ignoble means.

And, so, we take the field today
To find ourselves in how we play,
Out there on the field to be
Ourselves, a team, where all can see;
For nothing is but is revealed
And tested on the football field.

FIREPLACE

Where nothing was
But space alone
A fireplace is
Revealed in stone

Which shapes and garlands
The hearth's void –
The empty centre.
With what pride

The mason smiles
Who has let be
The perfect
Possibility.

MARY

Hail, full of grace
The Angel, uninvited,
Came to you in your own place
And your word united

Heaven and Earth, Above, Below
God needed you to say
Behold thy handmaid; had you said No
Where was God today?

A plucky girl, unmarried too
At the time of this conception –
What some would do to such as you
Does not bear mention.

You took your chance on God and life
No man before your will,
Queen of Heaven, common wife,
No precious, pale rel-

igious thing,
No prop for those who would
Impose themselves on everything
Not least your womanhood.

'I THIRST'

Midnight Mass one Christmas Eve,
The parish comes to pray –
A midnight of nostalgia
After a hard day;

For some have been preparing
Their Christmas at the sink,
And others have spent the day
Revelling in drink.

At Midnight Mass, the parish
Bows its head in prayer –
All but one have come along
In pious posture there.

All day, he's been drinking
In *The Corner House;*
When it comes to closing time
He buys, to carry out
For after mass, two bottles
Of Guinness Extra Stout.

And he stands there with the others
At the back wall of the church;
When it comes to the offertory,
Suddenly with a lurch

He staggers up the centre aisle
While the crowd looks on in shock,
Halting at the altar rails,
Careful not to drop

The bottles, he takes them out,
Plants them on the rails,
Faces the congregation,
Waves and then repairs

To the back and anonymity,
Hitches up his arse,
And some are shocked, and some amused
At this unholy farce.

But the Christ who thirsts on Calvary
Has waited all these years
For a fellow cursed with the cross of thirst
To stand him these few beers.

GOOD FRIDAY

Good Friday was the day of periwinkles:
The only day we got them – oh the treat!
An old lady and her son came up from Bally
With an ass-load. They were much more fun than
    meat.

They sold them by the handful to us children;
We took them home and pestered mom for pins.
They looked like snots when you fished them out. But
    Jesus!
That was some way to atone for all your sins!

We ate them by the fistful all that morning,
Receiving the essence of the tide.
The empty shells prefigured eggs for Easter.
At three o'clock the Christ was crucified.

The tang of winkles flavours my Good Fridays,
The emptiness familiar as the day.
The old woman's dead, her son too. Every weekend
The winkle man revives them on his tray.

IN MEMORIAM DANNY CUNNINGHAM
1912–1995

I take her to the funeral home –
She wants to see him dead;
She's not afraid – she rubs his hands
And then explores his head.

'He not wake up I rub him.
Look Daddy! He not move.
Where Danny, Dad?' she asks me.
'Danny's dead, my love'.

'Where Danny, Dad?' she asks again;
Then suddenly it's clear –
'The old Danny in the box', she says;
'The new one – he not here'.

MAY DALTON

The last word that was left to her was 'honour',
The stroke had taken all the rest away,
The one thing the void could not take from her
Was herself, and so she used to say
'Honour! Honour! Honour!' when you addressed her,
'Honour! Honour! Honour!' while her hand
Clutched her agitation. What depressed her
Was how those closest failed to understand
'Honour! Honour! Honour!', how our beaming
Was the beaming of an adult at a child:
'Honour! Honour! Honour!' had no meaning
For any but May Dalton. So we smiled.
A single word held all she had to say;
Enclosed within this word, she passed away.

SONNET TO BRENDA

I won't compare you to a summer's day,
The beaches all deserted in the rain –
Some way, this, to spend a holiday
(You're sorry now you didn't book for Spain).
No! The weather can't be trusted in these parts –
It's fickle as a false love's said to be;
I could get sentimental about hearts
But that's not my style. Poetry,
The only thing that's constant in my life,
The only thing I know that still is true
As my love remains for you, dear wife –
This, then, is what I'll compare to you.
The iambic heart that pulses in these lines
Measures out my love. And it still rhymes.

GAELTACHT

Here, for once, I didn't pine for home:
This was a world where language altered all;
Here Irish fitted like a poem –
In school, 'twas just a subject; here you'd fall
In love with being Irish: you were free
To learn the words of love not taught in school;
Oh! Irish was that girl at the *céilí* –
If you could only ask her out, not make a fool
Of yourself, and dance with her all night,
You'd learn the moods of Irish on her tongue;
She smiled at you, and oh! your head was light,
You danced with her and wheeled and waltzed and
     swung.
We danced all night, we didn't even kiss,
But this was love, was Irish, and was bliss.

Gaeltacht: (Irish) an Irish speaking district; the state of being
Irish
Céilí: (Irish) an Irish dancing session

DAN BREEN

For Fintan O'Toole

> There's a great gap between a gallous story and a dirty deed.
> *The Playboy of the Western World*

My Fight for Irish Freedom by Dan Breen –
I read it like a western; I'd pretend
To be a freedom fighter at thirteen –
It made a change from 'cowboys'; I'd spend
My spare time freeing Ireland in my head
Reliving his adventures one by one –
The policemen that he shot at Solohead,
Romance about the days spent on the run.

A nation born of romance and of blood,
Once ruled by men who killed for their beliefs,
Now a nation grown to adulthood
Losing faith in heroes, tribal chiefs.
Dan Breen is laid with the giants who held sway;
The gallous reads of dirty deeds today.

Gallous: a composite word, incorporating gallant, callous and gallows

KNOCKLONG

Oh, take me through the byroads
To those places named in song:
Along the road less travelled
Is the station of Knocklong
Where shots rang out for freedom
In nineteen and nineteen
With young Seán Hogan rescued
By Seán Treacy and Dan Breen.

As I drive to Tipperary
I recall the lore,
The War of Independence –
Here I park my car
On a road become a songline
And walk into the song
'The Rescue of Seán Hogan
At the Station of Knocklong'.

The station's now deserted,
Blocked up, overgrown
But not the gallous story,
An empire overthrown;
But I am overtaken

By the traffic on the road
Who hoot at this obstruction,
The progress I have slowed.

And so I take the burden
Of history and drive
Into Tipperary
Where I see New Ireland thrive;
But I'm glad I took the byroad
That led me into song –
Many roads to Tipperary
But only one Knocklong.

A PARENT'S LOVE

How close the sound of laughter and of tears!
My children watching *Dumbo* on TV
In the next room – are those wails or cheers?
At this remove their screaming worries me.

Do my children laugh or cry in the next room?
I check them out, and this is what I see –
No light illuminates the falling gloom,
Instead of watching *Dumbo* on TV,

High jinks on the sofa – they're both well,
I tick them off, their giggles fill and burst;
A parent's love knows all it needs of hell –
I hear them play and strangely fear the worst.

LISTENING TO *DESPERADOS WAITING FOR A TRAIN*

For John

How one thing always leads us to another!
I see you with your grandad once again
As you walk off from your father and your mother
To join him in the world of grown up men.
And yes, son, local folk called you his sidekick
As you walked around the village hand in hand,
No baby talk, 'twas adult stuff like politics
And it felt good to be treated like a man.
And though grandad's dead and everything is changing,
And you're growing up and soon will leave us, son,
And life's a past we're always rearranging,
When the kid walks with his hero in that song
I see you with your grandad once again
As you walk away to join the world of men.

ODE TO A PINT OF GUINNESS

'An Buachaill Caol Dubh', 'The Blonde in the Black Skirt'
You have given me life which I'd never have known,
For I was the shy one, inward and lonesome,
Fearful of people the years I was growing.

You came to me first in the years I was courting –
No girl would stay with me on lemonade;
You gave me fine words and a high reputation
For romance and laughter. At last I was made!
You came to me sad and you came to me happy –
There were parts of myself that lay unexplored,
But thanks to you, Guinness, there's nothing within us
That doesn't come out in thought, deed or word.

There are two kinds of truth, one drunk and one sober –
The ancient Egyptians knew this very well;
Before they'd pronounce, they'd examine it both ways –
The kind of good counsel I'd bottle and sell.

How different my life would be measured without you –
An egghead, I fear, with his nose in a book;
But now I can scan the pulse of my people
And the scholars will read it to get one last look
At the village before it has lost its own story,

The last place on earth for the wild and the free,
Ere we turn to designer beers, Beautiful Bodies!,
And we speak like bad actors speak on TV.

So here's to you, Guinness, muse and confuser –
You brought me to visions, you brought me to fart:
All the pain that you caused me was nothing at all, love,
To the knowledge you taught to this once-sober heart!

An Buachaill Caol Dubh: (Irish) 'The Dark Slender Boy', a syno-
nym for alcohol from the song of the same name by Seán Aerach
Ó Seanacháin (mid eighteenth century).

THE WOMAN OF THE HOUSE

The village – Ballygariff
Sometime in the past
Where the clock advanced for closing time
Is the only thing that's fast.

In her pub, Maggie Browne
(Browne's her maiden name)
Serves pints and whiskies to a group
Who've recently come home

On holiday from England,
They wear their Sunday best –
They're out to prove that exile
Does better than the rest

Who stay at home in Bally
And work that windswept hill
And so they dress in Sunday best
And flash big *twenty* bills.

Enter then Tom Guiney,
The singer, for a beer;
He's bought tobacco for himself,
Sugar, tea and flour

For his wife above in Barna,
He comes in for 'just the one'
But the exiles stand him porter
And demand of him a song.

All afternoon he sings for them;
At 'The Home I Left Behind'
The exiles back in Bally
Stare into black pints

For song is all that's left them
Of Bally long ago,
The past is all that's left them,
The only home they know.

Tom Guiney, man of honour,
Will stand his round
Though what's left in his pocket
Would hardly make a pound.

Nonetheless he calls for
A drink for the company –
'Twould never be said in Bally
He drank all day for free.

Maggie Browne sets up the drinks
And Tom must now admit
That he hasn't enough to pay for them –
Could she put it on the slate?

She does. And on with singing
But Maggie bides her time
And in a private moment
Takes Tom aside.

'Tom,' she says, 'You'll never
Call for a drink again
With no money in your pocket
For a crowd like them.

Call for your drink, Tom Guiney,
And when I put it up
If you've no money in your pocket
Let them take a sup

Or two and let them talk
And then come up to me
And ask me for the change
Of the *fiver* you gave me;

And Guiney, boy, you'll get it –
Never, never again
Let on that you've no money
To a crowd like them'.

The village – Ballygariff.
Time – the present. Now
We come to bury Maggie Browne;
We take and drink our stout –

We do this in memory
Of a woman we well know,
Exalter of the humble
In a singer long ago.

DAD

A man before his time, he cooked and sewed,
Took care of me – and Mammy in her bed,
Stayed in by night and never hit the road.
I remember well the morning she was dead
(I'd been living up in Arklow – my first job,
I hit the road in patches coming home),
He came down from her room, began to sob
'Oh Gabriel, Gabriel, Gabriel, Mam is gone'.
He held me and I told him not to cry
(I loved her too, but thought this not the place –
I went up to her room, cried softly 'Why?'
Then touched her head quite stiffly, no embrace).
Now when the New Man poses with his kid,
I think of all the things my father did.

IN MEMORY OF MY MOTHER

My mother lived for books though nearly blind.
An invalid, she read while she could see.
The only pleasure left her was her mind.

The books she read that pleased her were designed
To strip her life down to a clarity.
My mother lived for books though nearly blind

While I'd read all the comics I could find;
Confined to bed, she'd read 'good books' to me.
The only pleasure left her was her mind.

Delighting in the vision of her kind,
That second sight, the gift of poetry,
My mother lived for books though nearly blind,

Books I read from bookshelves that were lined
With poems she'd recite from memory.
The only pleasure left her was her mind.

And I remembered as I launched and signed
The first slim *Poems* of my maturity
How Mammy lived for books though nearly blind,
The only pleasure left to her, her mind.

SO WHAT IF THERE'S NO HAPPY ENDING?

In memoriam Michael Hartnett

So what if there's no happy ending?
Don't be afraid of the dark;
Open the door into darkness
And hear the black dogs bark.

Oh what a wonder is darkness!
In it you can view
The moon and stars of your nature
That daylight hid from you.

Open the door into darkness,
There's nothing at all to fear –
Just the black dogs barking, barking
As the moon and stars appear.

REQUIESCAT

He shouldered Mammy's coffin
And I was at his side,
A strong man in his fifties;
More than Mammy died

As we lowered her coffin,
My childhood ended then
As I stood beside my father
At her grave among the men.

We shouldered other coffins
These twenty years and more,
My father strong and steady
Though our shoulders would be sore.

And even last October
When his sister Nora died,
At eighty years he shouldered her
Still steady by my side.

He shouldered no more coffins –
When my aunt Mary died
And we went to lift her coffin,
My father stood aside.

His hand upon her coffin,
He followed up the aisle,
My father still beside me
Awhile.

His brothers now too feeble
To lift his coffin, when
My father died we wheeled him,
Myself and those old men.

And, as we lowered you, father,
A generation knew
That the time had come for passing on.
Now I inherit you.

IN THE WOODS

X on a tree trunk
Marks no buried treasure here
Children wonder why

*

A rotting tree stump
In the middle of the woods
Mushrooms with new life

*

Where there are nettles
There are dock leaves to heal us
In a spot nearby

TO MY D–28

Your body's unblemished
And sweetly you're strung,
A beauty I dreamed of
Since I was young,
But I'm middle aged
Losing hair, overweight,
And it's now you come to me,
My D–28.

As youngsters we dreamed
And talked of guitars,
We played out our crushes
On prized Yamahas,
And though we made music
When out on a date,
We wished we were playing
A D–28.

We played Epiphones, Yamahas,
Fenders – all good;
We played on them music
To suit every mood,
But deep down we dreamed
That sooner or late

We'd all find our very own
D–28.

The past becomes present,
The dream becomes true.
It was music I loved, dear
(I thought it was you);
You're all that I dreamed of
But now it's too late
For I'm pledged to another,
My D–28.

And still we make music
But now we both know
That there's no going back
To the long, long ago
For my road is taken,
I'm resigned to my fate,
My first and forever
D–28.

THE *DÍSEART*

A sign points to the *Díseart,*
A place of prayer and art –
An empty convent chapel
Whose private Harry Clarkes

(Twelve stained glass lancet windows)
Are public here today,
And some come here for beauty,
And some come here to pray.

Once I prayed in beauty
In the sanctuary of art –
How much was self deception?
What now is Harry Clarke?

What signifies the light
That's filtered in this place?
In this convent chapel
For some it still means grace.

But I leave the chapel,
It's given me no peace
(I'm through with self deception),
Face the teeming streets.

Nothing was transfigured
But I saw things in his light,
A beauty not sufficient
To transform my plight.

And yet, the heavens streaming
Through windows stained to art
Illuminate the darkness
In the chapel of my heart.

Díseart: (Irish) a retreat, a hermitage; a deserted place, a desert
Harry Clarke (1889–1931): was Ireland's outstanding stained
glass artist

COUNTRY LIFE

It's not so much that I'm out of fashion –
It's more that what I do was never 'in';
Oh sure, they paid lip-service, doled out rations
In some pie-eyed back-to-basics Gaelic dream.
And yes, we're still surviving, dancing, singing
At the crossroads where our betters turned away.
We choose to make a life here while they're clinging
To a past that we who live here know is fey.
And yes! they come on visits to the country
To see a past they say we should 'preserve'
As if we country folk were merely sentries:
When they come back, they get what they deserve –
A place that they no longer recognise,
A progress that they, tourists, must despise.

ON DECLINING A COMMISSION TO WRITE 200-WORD BIOGRAPHIES OF IRISH WRITERS FOR THEIR PORTRAITS IN A HOTEL

They put the writers' portraits on the wall –
It fills a space and elevates the tone;
Later, they might hold a festival
No matter that the writers wrote alone.
Everyone is at it, shops, hotels –
It brings in tourists seems to be the ploy;
Like wallpaper, it suits the decor well
And when the tourists come, we know they'll buy
Aran sweaters, crystal, Celtic kitsch,
Harmless stuff that tourists take away
(Budget stuff, up-market for the rich)
To remind them of their Irish holiday.
They've the writers where they want them – on the wall,
Backdrop to the muzak in the mall.

SCORN NOT THE BALLAD

Scorn not the ballad: it's the tale
Of lives like ours (and told without a fuss).
Sing it with a glass of flowing ale!
What's ours belongs to none, and all, of us.
No other verse can sing us like it does,
No other verse can wring out of the past
The strange, familiar melody that flows
Like truth from all who raise the singing glass.
Scorn not the ballad! Sing it out
In every public house, in every street;
It wasn't made for parlours - hear it shout!
Though sober as a sonnet, hear it beat.
You can't escape its rhythm, rough and rude;
You hum along not caring if you should.

ALZHEIMER'S DISEASE

'They're hanging me this evening', Mary says,
Or else it's a transplant she must have,
But her concern's observing the fast days
(The cares of childhood follow to the grave);
'Am I going to mass on Sundays?' she repeats
(How the good are frightened of their Church);
All we can do is comfort with deceit;
She's satisfied, and then begins to search
For biscuits, the indulgence of her life –
She'd eat them by the packet were she let,
A humble and obedient country wife;
Everything we tell her she'll forget,
But not the past – the past is as today
Where she was damned unless she would obey.

LASSIE

At ninety years he fell into a drain –
That's what John Bradley tells me from his bed
(Hospital plays tricks on old men's brains);
But for his dog, he tells me, he'd be dead.
How fact and fiction make us what we are –
He fell at home at bedtime in the dark
(The drain was years ago outside a bar);
His faithful dog had more sense than to bark –
She lay down on her master all night long,
Licked his face and wrapped him from the cold,
And when the ambulance came to take out John,
Lassie stayed and couldn't be consoled.
She guards his house and lets no stranger through –
When there's nothing left, love finds such things to do

KNOCKANURE CHURCH

A place of worship, simple and austere;
'Sixties architecture past its date.
I wonder what it is that draws me here
To a building local people seem to hate.
The church of their affection, knocked, made way
For the 'garage on the hill' in its design –
Bare brick, flat roof, no steeple, here I pray.
The spirit of this building's kin to mine.

My God's a God who strips me in this place –
No cover here, the lines are stark and spare;
Through the years, I've grown into this space
Where work of human hands raised art to prayer,
The same the builders raised up once at Chartres
But plainer here, an answer to my heart.

THE YELLOW BITTERN

Bitter, bird, it is to see
After all your spree, your bones stretched, dead;
Not hunger – No! by thirst laid low,
Flattened here on the back of your head.
It's worse than the ruin of Troy to me
To see you stretched among bare rock
Who never did harm nor treachery
Preferring water to finest hock.

My lovely bird, I sorely grieve
To see you stretched beside my path
Where you would swill and drink your fill
And from the puddle I'd hear your rasp.
Everyone warns your brother Cathal
That the drink will kill him, to stop and think;
But that's not so – observe this crow
Lately dead for want of drink.

My youthful bird, I'm so depressed
To see you stretched among the gorse
And the rats assembling for your waking
To sport and pleasure by your corpse.
And if you'd only sent a message
That you were in a fix, and dry,

I'd have split the ice upon Lake Vesey,
You'd have wet your mouth and your craw inside.

It's not for these birds that I'm mourning,
The blackbird, songthrush or the crane
But my yellow bittern, a hearty fellow,
Like me in colour, habit, name.
He was ever drinking, drinking
And so am I (they say I'm cursed) –
There's no drop I'm offered that I won't scoff
For fear that I might die of thirst.

'Give up the booze,' my darling begs me,
''Twill be your death.' Not so, I think;
I correct my dear's delusion –
I'll live longer the more I'll drink.
Look at this smooth-throated tippler
Dead from drought beside me here –
Good neighbours all, come wet your whistles
For in the grave you'll drink no beer.

Cathal Buí Mac Giolla Ghunna (c. 1690–1756)

CILL AODÁIN

Now spring is upon us, the days will be stretching,
And after *The Biddy* I'll hoist up and go;
Since I've decided, there'll be no returning
Till I stand in the middle of County Mayo.
In the town of Claremorris I'll spend the first evening,
And in Balla below it the first drinks will flow,
Then to Kiltimagh travel to spend a whole month there
Barely two miles from Ballinamore.

I set down forever that my spirit rises
Like fog as it scatters, as wind starts to blow
When I'm thinking of Carra or Balla below it,
Or Scahaveela or the plain of Mayo.
Cill Aodáin the fertile, where all fruits are growing –
Blackberries, raspberries, full-fruited each one,
And if I were standing among my own people
The years they would leave me, again I'd be young.

Antoine Ó Reachtabhra (Raftery) (c. 1784–1835)

The Biddy: Saint Brigid's Day, the first day of spring
Cill Aodáin: the poet's place of birth

DÓNALL ÓG

Dónall Óg, if you cross the ocean
Take me with you and don't forget
On fair day and market you'll have a present
And a Greek king's daughter in your bed.

But if you leave, I have your description –
Two green eyes and a fair-haired poll,
A dozen plaits in your yellow ringlets
Like a cowslip or a garden rose.

Late last night, the dog announced you
And the snipe announced you in the marsh that's deep
While all alone you walked the woodlands,
May you be wifeless till you find me.

You made a promise, but a lie you told me,
That you'd be before me at the fold;
I gave a whistle and three hundred calls for you
But a bleating lamb your absence told.

You promised me, and it wasn't easy,
Silver masts and a golden fleet,
A dozen towns and all with markets
And a lime-white mansion by the sea.

You promised me and it impossible
You'd give me gloves made from skin of fish,
You'd give me shoes made out of bird-skin
And a suit made of the dearest silk.

With me, Dónall, you'd do far better
Than with a haughty lady puffed with pride,
I'd milk your cows and I'd do your churning
And I'd strike a blow for you at your side.

Oh my grief! and it isn't hunger,
Lack of food or drink or sleep
That leaves me here so thin and haggard
But from a young man's love that I am sick.

I saw the youth in the morning early
On horseback riding down the road,
But he didn't approach or entertain me,
I cried my fill as I turned for home.

When I go to the Well of Sorrows
I sit down and wail and sigh
When I see them all there but my darling
With the amber shadow on his cheekbone high.

'Twas on a Sunday my love I gave you,
The one before last Easter Day,
I on my knees as I read the Passion
But my two eyes gave my love away.

'Don't speak with him', my mother warned me,
'Today, tomorrow or any day'.
A fine time, now, to give such warning,
Locking the stable when the thief's away.

I beg you, mother, give me to him
And give him all in the world you own
Even if you have to beg for alms
But don't deny what I implore.

This heart of mine is black as sloes are,
Black as a coal is in a forge,
Or the print of a shoe in the whitest hall is,
And above my laughter, my heart is sore.

You took my east from me, you took my west,
Before and after I've lost to you,
You took the sun from me, you took the moon,
And I fear you've taken my God, too.

Author unknown

THE BOG-DEAL BOARD

I'd wed you, join without cow or coin
Or dowry too,
My own! my life! with your parents' consent
If it so pleased you;
I'm sick at heart that we are not,
You who make my heart to soar,
In Cashel of Munster with nothing under us
But a bog-deal board.

Walk, my love, and come with me
Away to the glen,
And you'll find shelter, fresh air by the river
And a flock bed;
Beneath the trees, beside us
The streams will rush,
The blackbird we'll have for company
And the brown song-thrush.

The love of my heart I gave you –
In secret too;
Should it happen in the course of life
That I and you
Have the holy bond between us

And the ring that's true,
Then if I saw you, love, with another,
I'd die of grief for you.

Author unknown

BROWN EYES

These brown eyes I see are hers
Now in her son's head,
It was a thing most beautiful
That you inherited;

It was a meeting privileged
With her mind and body too,
For a thousand years would pass so swift
If they but looked at you.

Because those eyes belong to her
It's strange that he has them,
I'm ashamed to face her now because
They happened in a man.

When she and they were one to me
Little did I think
Those eyes would change to masculine
That spoke so womanly.

Where is the source of madness
That's any worse than this?
Do I have to change my dialogue
Now that they are his?

She wasn't the first to see with them
Any more than he
Nor will he be the last
Who will wear them.

Is this all there is of eternity
That something of us lives on
Becoming masculine and feminine
From the mother to the son?

Seán Ó Ríordáin (1917–1977)

A CHANGE

'Come over,' said Turnbull, 'and look at the sorrow
In the horse's eyes.
If you had hooves like those under you,
There would be sorrow in your eyes.'

And 'twas plain that he knew the sorrow so well
In the horse's eyes,
And he wondered so deeply that he dived in the end
Into the horse's mind.

I looked at the horse then that I might see
The sorrow in his eyes,
And Turnbull's eyes were looking at me
From the horse's mind.

I looked at Turnbull and looked once again
And there in Turnbull's head –
Not Turnbull's eyes, but, dumb with grief,
Were the horse's eyes instead.

Seán Ó Ríordáin (1917–1977)

CHRISTMAS EVE

With candles of angels the sky is now dappled,
The frost on the wind from the hills has a bite,
Kindle the fire and go to your slumber,
Jesus will lie in this household tonight.

Leave all the doors wide open before her,
The Virgin who'll come with the child on her breast,
Grant that you'll stop here tonight, Holy Mary,
That Jesus tonight in this household may rest.

The lights were all lighting in that little hostel,
There were generous servings of victuals and wine
For merchants of silk, for merchants of woollens
But Jesus will lie in this household tonight.

Máire Mhac an tSaoi (b. 1922)

VIETNAM LOVE SONG

They said we were shameless
celebrating our love
with devastation all around us

the hawk hovering in the air
awaiting the stench of death

they said that these were our own
that this was the funeral of our own people
that we should at least be solemn
even if we were not mourning

but we
we are like the weather
        especially the sun
we don't pay much attention
to these happenings any longer

everything decays in the heat of the sun
after death

and it wasn't we who killed them
but you

we could have stayed on the field of slaughter
but the sad faces of the soldiers
made us laugh
and we chose a soft spot by the river

Caitlín Maude (1941–1982)

CAPTIVITY

I am an animal

a wild animal
from the tropics
        famous
        for my beauty

I would shake the trees of the forest
once
with my cry

but now
I lie down
and observe with one eye
the lone tree yonder

people come in hundreds
every day
who would do anything
for me
but set me free

Caitlín Maude (1941–1982)

THE PURGE

For Arthur and Vera Ward

Hartnett, the poet, might as well be dead,
enmeshed in symbol – the fly in the web;
and November dribbles through the groves
and metaphors descend on him in droves:
the blood-sucked symbols – the sky so blue,
the lark, the kiss, and the rainbow too.
This syrupy drivel would make you puke.

The monarch now of an inch of vision,
I'll not fall down for indecision
but banish for now and forever after
the rusty hinges, the rotten rafters,
the symbols, the cant, the high allusion
that reduce the white mind to confusion.
Inspiration comes and the poet is left
with the empty rattle of discarded shells,
the husks of beetles piled up dead –
his poem spoiled by stupid talk
that sucks the blood of an ancient craft
like a bloated tick on a mongrel's balls.

I must purge my thought and flay my diction
or else suffer that fierce affliction –

my poems only wind and bombast
having lost their human language.

Pleasant the young poet's dance with books
but the old poet's advance should be rebuffed –
the mummer in the tinker's shawl,
the garrulous brass-thief, the jackdaw,
the beat-up chair at the carpenter's,
and the scabby mouths of idle whores.
Bad cess to him who first compared
the poet's rhymes to the singing bird –
he insulted plumage, he insulted verse.
May Egypt shit him from a swallow's arse.

The fledgeling's sweet, but it's insipid
to hear the chaffinch act the meadow-pipit.
Look at all our native birds
in stinking cages dung-floored;
their nests, the cast-offs of the age
where the birds moult in frightful rage.
They court and welcome the louse of fame
and, dying old, they die in vain:
ignorant, with nothing left
but dregs and leavings. Outside the nest
the dance is stopped, the din consigned
to empty souls, to vacant minds.

My uncle's ribs are clattering
in my pocket; and hear again –
on the stairs the cacophony
of granny's skull (this symphony
of bones) – priests' and brothers' cries –
the wounded soul in my father's eyes:
the course whisper of my youth.
My ancestors march in dark pursuit:
Uncle Hate and Auntie Guilt,
I adore you both and your ancient quilts:
a poet must be true to his sources.
He wears a necklace of his mother's teeth;
with his brother's skin, his book's bound neat;
he's a curer of skins, a burier of corpses.
An eternal penance, this opening of graves –
the poets in the graveyards always with spades
and shovels fighting over bones –
one shines his sister's kneecap's dome,
one scrapes maggots from his mother's womb.
Each poem an elegy, a litany, or lament;
each line morbid with the hideous dead;
and hung around each poet's neck
are the tanned relics of his father's scrotum.

History is only selected time –
there are poems a-plenty, but the editor's bribed,
the king's lackey with the fool's mind.

History is only for the man displaced –
it's the hump on his back, his *raison d'être* –
he converses daily with the great.
Isn't it grand to meet with Plato,
or drink in the pub with Emmet, the *craythur;*
or often with Christ to discuss your views
('tis a great solace to an author
when he thinks of the death of a million Jews.)
Oh, 'tis our hump and our very substance,
our healing and our holy ointment:
our minds think only (being so impoverished)
of quietness, and crookedness, and corpses.
History is a mere poultice
drawing pus from the hopeless:
it stains the white mind with its themes;
it entices the dark to the *céilí*
to spin, to swing, to escape again
back to the corner with lonely mind.
And greatness palls with Christ and Plato
and the poet is left with his empty soul
like a chalice lonely beneath the soil.

Like mouse-fur in a cat's mouth
or a blood-clot seeking a brain,
the white myths are stalking
the old poets' veins:
Icarus, Meadbh and Christ –

yes, the Christ who died
to free the world of mythologies
is himself mythologised.
These are scabs of knowledge, and cankers in the groin,
the leeches of the soul sucking strong.
When we're tired and frightened
and when poetry dies
we plant the white ghosts in the scorched garden.
We believe that they're alive –
the dead forever dead, except in our silly minds.
Zeus and Venus, fables from the hedge
schools, fill us and take the edge
from thirst and poem-hunger: we're now well fed
and the university listens to our belch.
Mars with his shield incites, amused,
when the land of old soldiers is badly ruled
and aflame with discontented youth.
Goodbye to frippery, to jewellery, the toy;
to Jove and Gráinne and Daedalus, goodbye;
to Churches hung with miracles
like sheep's afterbirth by holy wells.

A poet must master words, must learn his trade;
must be schooled in poetry, know how poems are made:
every poem in the world, its song and make.
Avoid labels and lepers' bells,
avoid the pedant pedagogical:

no poet is without colour, without stone, without chord.
But colour and granite won't yield to words,
the impoverished poet's syllables.
The poet's fugues add wind to wind
and wreck the work of greater men,
but white and empty, day and night,
we dose ourselves with others' thought
and stumble blithely to the heap of husks
and carouse safely in the pub –
we're no bees replete in the hive
but drunken wasps in the height of horrors
from sucking too much vinegar.

And always at night antique Tradition,
lizard-infested, screams its mission:
'assonance! alliteration!' and 'free verse!'
its retinue of poets shove up its arse
their ancient airs and metaphors.
But the pig is as its master
and, though the sheet be loused, dirt-plastered,
the skin beneath doesn't need
the rowdy rabble's rotten feed.
It's not a static system, but an accumulating change
that its priests don't recognise (those beggars of fame)
who stuff its maw with people
and poems till the creature
farts phrases fragrant to the sky –

an incense they find agreeable, if high!
Avoid the silliness of glens
and their decaying placenames;
avoid the broken walls, the gorse's assonance.
Shun that sham, Tradition,
or 'twill welt your skin's condition;
it will smother the poet's vision
till the butter of your songs
is lost in bitter sloe-jam.

I am the grave of hope and the tomb of truth,
swiller of fame, gulper of residues.
The systems of great men will never mend
my heart's drop-down, the leak of sentiment.
I construct myself with Plato's ears,
Hegel's thumb, Freud's beard,
Nietzsche's 'tache and Bergson's teeth
to make my body whole, complete.
I add Buddha to the crush
and Lao Tsu's teachings are a must:
but a pain in my belly upsets my powers
and my body explodes in a rain of flowers,
and down I come with a shower of poets –
oh, they're some flowers, these perfumed oafs
with juniper of Aristotle, bogcotton of Kant,
sage of Schopenhauer, arrogant.
Here in a wood among stem and branch

like a child lost at a hurling match,
I hear the cheering of lusty throats
and see only the hems of coats.

Oh, I am Frankenstein and his creature
made of spittle, and bits and pieces.

The old story – the poet and God
conversing together – that's all wrong.
There is no poetic pantheon
though the nine muses keep him going.
When he dies, his god dies with him,
and cancer-, and liver-, and heart-condition:
the poet's mind and balls die with him,
and fear of the void dies also with him:
the goose-down quilts fade in the air –
each man is Christ and his cross waits there.
No poet ever spoke to God
though he turns to Christ when he goes mad.
He walks under heaven like a simple *eejit*
and goes to the well to talk to Bridget.
Courting her grace, and seeking to kiss her, he
is no poet but an emissary.
He abandons country, he abandons rhymes,
as when I myself had a white mind;
and God can't blame me, because I tried
and the stars rained spittle in my eyes.

Poet-protector, poet-mother
lord of symbols, the metaphor.
A world without metaphor is a world dirty:
who sees it thus, dies at thirty.
Listen well to what I set down –
I'm forty years, I've seven cats drowned.
I have seen their tortured eyes,
their manic teeth like stars gone wild.
They clawed a bracelet on my hand
as death bubbled in the bath.
I dived to the ash of a likely pub
and the cats' teeth became black from soot.
Metaphor, mother, I'll be your sire:
give me your poison, give me your light.
I'll break you in, but I'll be your horse;
I'll hold the reins, but you'll be the jock.
Tired metaphors go to roost
and the dung piles up beneath their toes,
same old roost, same old symbol, same old poet:
no wonder the crows are all insane
stripping the trees and banging against them –
for metaphors now we're madly searching,
full of carrion: cackling and barking –
the crow-choir echoes what I set down:
'forty years and seven cats drowned'.

Imagine a world with nothing but poems,
desert-naked and bare-boned:
with nothing but swans and lilies and roses –
such a meagre fauna and flora.
All the foliage in technicolour,
dwarf and giant, joy and squalor.
If poets celebrate the world's soul
and the rare and wonderful they extol,
where's the mention of the plover?
Where's the nest of the water dipper?
If no bird sang but philomel,
and nothing was but sunrise, sunset,
the world we live in would be hell.
We're the boys who adore freedom
wanting only the praise of people:
we're the boys who fatten geese
to swell their livers for our feast.
We lost the election for our party,
the rags we wear make tailors narky.
We promise you silk and we give you cotton,
we fill the world with wrens from top to bottom.
The poet is only his collected verse,
and all he was is contained in books:
His poetry is his true memorial –
other than that, mere fables and stories.
Our viaticum is knowledge
and death wants nothing from us

but ourselves and our knowledge.
The brave man spends knowledge freely
or else grows frightened, growing lonely;
and the straws fall that he stole from others –
his roof leaks on him. He shudders:
his bloated soul no more will hunger
and his once white mind is white no longer
and the thatch hardens, and the lights are smothered.
To die without knowledge of yourself
is the worst darkness, the worst hell:
to bequeath your truth to humanity
is the only immortality.
A jackdaw's death is a death, without question –
a nest torn down by the storms of autumn.

Statement is castrated verse –
a cry, a slogan – so we've heard:
the hymn of the pompous clerk.
Once our country was *Róisín Dubh:*
today it's a warlord, a stoat with a hood,
a sandy beach with an oil-soaked bird.
Of slogans now you can take your pick –
not poems or songs but rhetoric.
Where verse is treacherous, 'tis fitting and right
for the poet to turn fighter with an armalite.
A poem in prison isn't worth a fart –

won't dent a helmet, won't stop a shot:
won't feed a soul when the harvest rots,
won't put food in hungry pots.
Famine and war to all historians!
May pop stars roar our ballads glorious!
Justice is the poet's land:
he has no family but a load
of dreams to sting, and coax, and goad
with words as worthless as tin cans.
May heavy boots stomp on the head
that forgets the danger of being understood.

Your human being is a funny bloke
believing in god and the devil both;
secretly whispering early and late:
'life and death, and love and hate.'
Long years have closed our eyes,
'war will come' and 'thank God' we cry –
the clergy have taught us to be shy
preaching 'the just war' and 'love!'
Oh, they doped us with their drug –
their Universal God Above.
The Universal made us infantile,
cut our literature down to size
and pagan dawnsong is Christianised.
Like cowards we follow with our sweet scribble
always in search of a stone-age nipple.

War will come for we believe in war:
it's a great consolation to know this for sure –
it's our choice of nipple, this barefaced warring:
it's Universal, common, ordinary.

Butter my hand with reputation,
spread the terrible jam of my friends' ruination.
'Tis seldom you see a poet honest:
he strokes the foal that praises his sonnets –
that brute would bite – keep your hand far from it.
The tribe, the people, and the race
are rightly blamed and rightly praised;
but there's no friend in that spooky parlour –
just sheets like shrouds over tables, over spectres.
A poet can fill his life
with family, friends, his kids, the wife,
but none can answer his overwhelming question:
how poets exist with no attention.
Loner or gregarious, sane or mad,
worn from nourishing the cuckoo in his head;
expert in envy, lord of the absurd,
attracting every jibe and snigger in the world:
strewing pride and presents among the crowds
beside the grotesque tables and the shrouds,
in the parlour of his head mourning and weeping –
homeless, friendless among his people.

Poetry is a rat trapped: it cannot live
in the fangs of allusion, the fangs of adjective,
poisonous both, especially the latter,
sweet as the Munster thrushes' chatter,
their songs like goat-shit on a drum.
The adjective produces a sickly noun,
and all my rhymes are maternity homes
where nouns are patients and mothers both,
and my Lord Adjective is outside
waiting his chance of another ride.
Cut 'em down, and dry, and turn 'em,
and make a heap of 'em and burn 'em
and through the smoke, our names you'll see:
no tree is green – a tree is a tree.
A tree is a name, and real too:
green is only a point of view.
But be careful when the scythe swings
for the stubble is full of war-shocked limbs.
Give poetry a hand, undo its collar,
give the noun air, or it will smother.

A critic floundered in a poem once
for want of signposts, the poor dunce.
He crushed each subtlety underfoot
and wept, hearing their brittle crunch.
He prayed to God that he might see;
he invoked the ghosts of the university.

'Straight ahead,' came the blessed answer,
'to line twenty-nine, and look for Dante',
and, released, he praised the poem, the chancer.
He saw no polish, or craft, or care
nor the subtle power of the poet aware –
only that ugly signpost there.
His compass was of no account
in a place that had no north or south.
What's a critic, in the name of Bridget,
or can any 'objective correlative' gauge it?

So, what is left when the piper ceases?
Dregs, spit, echoes, treacle.

There's still a problem, all said and done:
the poem that lives, will it be human?
I break my dictum – it's not a rule
but a harness on me, poetry's mule.

I am a conspiracy of one.
I'm humble, arrogant; when all is done,
my rules are easily broken:
I fill ten books to say: let nothing be spoken.
Serve the eclipse, keep a slice of the moon,
be a small light, be an exception too.
Suck the plum, spit out the stone –
it will land on dung

and a thousand trees will grow.
Don't be competitive: all we have is poems,
things not answerable
to leader or pope.

This is Ireland, and I'm myself.
I preach the gospel of non-assent.
Love and art is the work I want
as empty as a dipper's nest,
whiter than a goose's breast –
the poet's road with no milestone on it,
a road with no wayside stop upon it,
a road of insignificant herbs
welling quietly from every hedge.

Mícheál Ó hAirtnéide (Michael Hartnett) 1941–1999

Róisín Dubh: an allegorical name for Ireland

HERE AT *CAISEAL NA* gCORR STATION

For Michael Davitt

Here at *Caiseal na gCorr* Station
I discovered my hidden island,
my refuge, my sanctuary.
Here I find myself in tune
with my fate and environment.
Here I feel permanence
as I look at the territory of my people
around the foot of Errigal
where they've settled
for more than three hundred years
on the grassy mountain pastures
from *Mín 'a Leá* to *Mín na Craoibhe.*
Here before me, open
like a book,
is this countryside now
from *Doire Chonaire* to *Prochlais.*
Above and below, I see the holdings
farmed from the mouth of wilderness.
This is the poem-book of my people,
the manuscript they toiled at
with the ink of their sweat.
Here every enclosed field is like a verse
in the great poem of land reclamation.
I read this epic of diligence now

in the green dialect of the holdings,
understanding that I'm only fulfilling my duty
when I challenge the Void
exactly as my people challenged the wilderness
with diligence and devotion
till they earned their prize.
Here I feel the worth of poetry.
I feel my *raison d'être* and importance as a person
as I become the pulse of my people's heart
and from this certainty comes peace of mind.
My desires are tamed, my thoughts mellow,
contradictions are cancelled on the spot.

Cathal Ó Searcaigh (b. 1956)

A BRADDY COW

For Liam Ó Muirthile

He got fed up, I'd swear,
of the loneliness that constantly seeps down
through the rolling hills, through the valleys
sluggish as a hearse;
of the lazy hamlets of the foothills
empty of youth as of earth;
of the old warriors, of the sodbusters
who turned to red-sod the peaty soil
and who deafened him pink, year-in, year-out,
bragging of the old sods of the past;

of the small, white bungalows, ugly
as dandruff in the sedgy headlands of the glen;
of the young trapped in the cage of their fate
like wild animals who have lost their cunning;
of the three sorrows of storytelling in the misery
of the unemployed, of low spirits,
of the backwardness, of the narrowmindedness of both
    sides of the glen,
of the fine birds below in *Ruairi*'s
who stirred the man in him
but who couldn't care less about his lusting;

of tribal boundaries, of ancient household ditches,
of pissing his frustration at race and religion
that walled him in.
He got fed up of being fettered in the glen
and, bucking like a braddy cow one spring morning,
he cleared the walls and hightailed away.

Cathal Ó Searcaigh (b. 1956)

A braddy cow: a thieving, trespassing cow

TO JACK KEROUAC

For Séamus de Bláca

> The only people for me are the mad ones,
> the ones who are mad to live, mad to talk,
> mad to be saved, desirous of everything at
> the same time, the ones who never yawn or
> say a commonplace thing but burn,
> burn like fabulous yellow roman candles.
>
> From On the Road

Leafing through your books tonight, a breeze of memory
from every page,

My youth was resurrected, and, rising in me, I felt the
dreamy beat that imitated you in the early 1970s.

1973. I was hooked on you. Day after day, your work
was a shot of inspiration that lit up my mind and
stretched my imagination.

Then it wasn't *Mín 'a Leá* or *Fána Bhuí* I'd see but the
plains of Nebraska or the grasslands of Iowa.

And when the blues descended it wasn't the *Bealtaine*
byways that lay ahead but the open freeway of
America.

'Hey man you gotta stay high,' I'd say to my friend
as we freaked through *Cill Ulta*'s California or *Fál
Charrach*'s Frisco.

Your book is shut on my breast but beneath the skin that
is the cover your heart is throbbing in the muscle of
every word.

Oh man! I feel it again, those highs on the Himalayas
of youth:

From coast to coast we coasted, naive, vivacious, reckless

Hitch-hiking on our pilgrimage from New York to
Frisco and from there to Mexico City,

A mad beat to our lives. Inspired. Bombing down high-
ways in hot Cadillacs, bombed out of our minds on
Benzedrine.

We crossed borders and broke through to dreams.

We celebrated every turn on our life's highway, binges
and brotherhood from Brooklyn to Berkeley, booze,
bop and Buddhism; the sages of Asia; envelopes from
eternity on the Sierras; marijuana and mysticism in
Mexico; crazy visions in Bixby Canyon.

We made an Orpheus of every orifice.

Oh I remember it all, Jack, the talk and the quest.

You were the quick-eyed bard on the road seeking
perfection, seeking heaven.

And though there's no short-cut to the Gods, so they
say, you harnessed and electrified the Niagara of
your mind with dope and divinity

And in that furious moment a light was generated that
    granted you a glimpse of eternity
And that guided you home, I hope, on the day of your
    death to Whitman, Proust and Rimbaud.

My own road is ahead of me ... *a road that ah zigzags
all over creation. Yeah man! Ain't nowhere else it can
go. Right!'*
And some day on the road of old age and rheumatism,
Or sooner maybe,
I'll arrive at the crossroads of fate, and death will be there
    before me,
A gentle guide to lead me beyond the border
And then, goddammit Jack, we'll both be hitch-hiking
    in eternity.

Cathal Ó Searcaigh (b. 1956)

MY BLACKHAIRED LOVE

My blackhaired love, my dear, dear, dear,
Our kiss re-opens Christ's wounds here;
But close your mouth, don't spread the word:
We offend the Gospels with our love.

You plague the local belles, my sweet,
They attempt to coax you with deceit,
But you'd prefer my lonely kiss,
You hugging me to bring to bliss.

Lay your head, my dear, dear, dear,
Lay your head on my breast here;
I'll close my mouth, no detail break –
I'd deny the gospels for your sake.

Cathal Ó Searcaigh (b. 1956)

THE CELEBRANT'S A CRITIC

The celebrant's a critic or he's lost
The soul of his own people in a blind
Elevation of his parish at the cost
Of putting the obnoxious from his mind.
They shit on us, these upstarts who return
To the pubs in which they drank; I know their breed -
They boast to old acquaintance as they burn
With all the ostentation of their greed.
Fuck off with your money as you stand
Buying off misfortune at the bar;
I'm a celebrant and though you shake my hand
And act as if in friendship, this is war.
I stand up for my people, mind them well,
I know your kind, your money. Go to hell.

THE BALLAD OF RUDI DOODY

A song

My name is Rudi Doody
From Kildeboodybeg,
I'm one week out from Ireland,
Here in Winnipeg;
I'm off to make me fortune
In a land beyond the sea
But I'll ne'er forget where'er I roam
What me mother said to me.

'Goodbye Rudi Doody,
Off to Winnipeg;
Remember Moody Doody
In Kildeboodybeg;
Write a letter now and then
And send us the few pound –
The more we get, the more we want
Till we're six foot underground'.

Then one day a letter came
From far off Winnipeg
Announcing Rudi Doody
To Kildeboodybeg;
He came all rings and biros,

And boasted in the pub
That he could buy the whole damn place
And give every man the sub.

He spent three weeks in Ireland,
Stood all his mates a round,
Staggered to the butcher shop
For the best of steak in town;
And then, the three weeks over,
He packed his case again,
And the cock crew in the mornin'
As he boarded on the plane.

Meanwhile back in Ireland
In Kildeboodybeg,
His mates all toast this *dacent* man
In far off Winnipeg;
But as the years roll onward,
He comes back less and less
For the kids at home drink with their own –
They don't know who he is.

Goodbye Rudi Doody,
Off to Winnipeg;
Remember Moody Doody
In Kildeboodybeg;
Write a letter now and then

And send us the few pound –
The more we get, the more we want
Till we're six foot underground.

The more we get, the more we want
Till we're six foot underground.

MAIRG NACH FUIL 'NA DHUBHTHUATA

After the Irish of Dáibhí Ó Bruadair (c. 1625–1698)

Oh to be pig-ignorant
With money in the Bank
Among these boors and upstarts,
Their tabloid *Daily Wank*.

Oh to be pig-ignorant
Then I wouldn't see
The Sunday Poem passed over
For the strippers on page three.

A LOCAL MURDER

They all know the murderer
But there's a worse disgrace –
To be an informer
In your native place.

One summer's day a stranger,
Innocent of this code,
Stops for a drink of water
At a cottage on the road.

Suspicious of the stranger,
Yet country courtesy
Invites him to her kitchen;
They small-talk, he and she,

And, looking out the window,
He admires the view;
When it's time to take his leave of her,
He asks, as one will do,

What that nearby hill is called.
Standing at her door
'As true as God, good man,' she says,
'I never saw it before'.

THE DAY CHRIST CAME TO MOYVANE

He came to fix umbrellas,
Kettles, basins, pans;
The squad car turned in my yard
And jumped the tinker man –

'What are you doing? What's your name?'
'Get going out of here';
The tinker man walked down the drive,
My dog snapped at his heels.

But the tinker man was used to dogs,
He just kept walking on,
And as he walked he whistled
And was gone.

The guard was doing his duty –
There had been reports
Of travellers casing houses.
I'd been robbed before,

So I thanked the guard and offered him
A beer, a cup of tea,
And as we talked, the tinker man
Walked farther away from me.

BEFORE THE WORD 'FUCK' CAME TO COMMON USE

Before the word 'fuck' came to common use
(Even toddlers going to play school know it now),
Before the lid was raised on child abuse,
We said that we were innocent. But how?
We heard the whispers and we went along
Protecting those who were above the law
In a world we eulogise ('knew right from wrong'),
A world nostalgia paints without a flaw.
Before the word 'fuck' came to common use
We were children and our masters ran the show ...
Guilty as condemned, it's no excuse
To plead that in the past we didn't know.
Before the word 'fuck' came to common use
Children mattered less than their abusers.

THE MISSION MAGAZINES

They're in decline, the *Africa,*
Mission Outlook, The Far East,
The divine word is dying
With its nuns and priests.

This testament to piety,
These little acts of hope
With pictures of the mission lands,
Their saints, an ageing pope

Are in decline like religion
In the disillusioned west,
They leave a void behind them
And our defining quest

For eternal truth and beauty
Is consumed like booze
In headlong self-destruction
We call our right to choose.

They're in decline, these pieties,
Relics of the past
In an age of self expression
Where nothing's said to last.

ON HEARING JOHNNY CASH'S
AMERICAN RECORDINGS

The great ones have the courage to believe,
The courage to go naked if so called,
To pare life back to where things don't deceive;
Let those ashamed of feeling be appalled,
These simple songs of love and death ring true
In an age when we're afraid to show the heart –
'Whatever you say, say nothing', this in lieu
Of a creed that years ago joined prayer and art.
We say nothing and mean nothing now that we
Lose belief and, cynics in our loss,
Look down on the believer, this poetry –
The gospel of a soul that takes its cross,
Songs a life has earned or else are trash,
Salvation, suffered, sung by Johnny Cash.

HIS LAST PINT

He came into the village one last time
Defying cancer by an act of will
As he came into the village in his prime.

He left with me as his clock began to chime
Nine o'clock; swallowing a pill,
He came into the village one last time.

We stopped at Kincaid's Bar; he couldn't climb
Out of my car until I helped him. Still,
As he came into the village in his prime,

He walked in unsupported, and I'm
Certain that the drinkers felt a chill
As he came into the village one last time.

He called for a Carlsberg and lime
Too weak now for the Guinness that he'd swill
When he came into the village in his prime.

But the cancer couldn't take his state of mind:
From the tap of life the dying drank his fill –
He came into the village one last time
As he came into the village in his prime.

THE MOTHER

Forced to view his body –
Her guerrilla son
Shot dead in an ambush
By an occupier's gun;

Forced to view his body
In the workhouse where,
Lest there should be reprisals,
She could show no mother's care;

Forced to view his body,
She denied she knew her son
Then left him to an unmarked grave.
That's how the war was won.

MUNSTER FOOTBALL FINAL 1924

Nothing polarises like a war,
And, of all wars, a civil war is worst;
It takes a century to heal the scars
And even then some names remain accursed.
The tragedies of Kerry, open wounds –
John Joe Sheehy on the run in 'twenty-four,
The Munster Final in the Gaelic Grounds:
There's something more important here than war.
John Joe Sheehy, centre-forward, republican,
Con Brosnan, free state captain, centre-field;
For what they love, they both put down the gun –
On Con's safe conduct, Sheehy takes the field.
In an hour the Kerry team will win.
Sheehy will vanish, on Brosnan's bond, again.

A FOOTBALLER

Homage to John Quane

He could have played with better
But he chose his own;
Playing with his county
He'd never carry home

The trophy all aspire to
But that's not why he played:
If he played with another county
He'd feel he had betrayed

Himself, his art, his people,
So he plays out his career
Away from the glare of headlines.
And yet sometimes you'll hear

From followers of football
The mention of his name.
It's enough that they believe in him,
His way, his truth, his game.

POEM FOR NESSA, FIVE YEARS OLD

She brings me a pale strawberry
While I'm sitting on the loo,
The last one in the garden,
Says, 'Dad, this is for you'.

I don't know what I'd do without her –
There simply is no place
That she won't come and find me,
A smile upon her face.

For Nessa always finds things –
No matter what is lost,
Nessa's sure to find it.
She's found me in the past

When I've been lost and lonely,
Nowhere to lay my head,
She's brought me hope – like strawberries.
Who cares if they're not red!

POEM FOR JOHN

A bucket on his head, a pretend soldier
Wearing Mammy's boots that reached above
  his knee ...
He remembers this quite clearly now he's older –
The magic world he lived in, turning three.
He'd go to bed sitting on my shoulder,
His *Daddy Doodle,* oh so proud of me!
It's not that what's between us has grown colder –
To grow apart is part of being free.

I love you, son, as on the day you came
Into my life, a baby who would need
All I could give, my love, a home, a name,
My word made flesh though not born of my seed.
Tonight you put your Teddy from your bed –
The magic wanes, the world looms ahead.

A WIDOWER

They thought to make you marry when she died;
Accounts of matches came from women who
Would share your life should you take one as bride,
But, constant as your love for her was true,
You lived alone for nearly thirty years
In the home you made with Mam, an invalid.
I remember once you told me over beers
The reason why you did the things you did.
You said you'd bring no other to your life
Fearing I, your only child, would be upset.
Not so, Dad: caring for your wife
You knew the love that lovers don't forget.
The others who would wed you came too late.
A love like yours would take no other mate.

HOME

My family are dying one by one,
My uncles and my aunts – just Peg now left:
The ones who, returning to Moyvane,
Brought England with them in the way they dressed.
They'd travel home from Shannon on the bus
(We'd no cars back then to make the trip),
Though a lifetime 'over', they spoke the same as us,
Still the same old Kerry accent rough and rich.
They never lost their Kerry: they'd no need
To lose themselves in England, or to pine
For Ireland lost as they passed on their seed;
My cousins are English, and our line
Still comes home to visit: they belong,
A people and a place that still are one.

THE FITZS COME TO TOWN

Those sultry summer nights in Dinny Mack's,
The Fitzs home from England; the whole clan
Singing, dancing, drinking for the crack.
Those nights were the talk of half Moyvane.
Musicians came and played till closing time,
The Fitzs danced their old-time sets again,
Drink flowed like talk that's loosed by beer and wine
And teens accepted shandies from the men.
Those sultry summer nights in Dinny Mack's
All were welcome among the Fitzs who
Brought the summer with them and relaxed
Who never shirked when there was work to do.
And Dinny Mack would stand us the odd round
Saying "Tis better than the Carnival when the Fitzs
    come to town'.

The crack: revelry, fun, high spirits – often Gaelicised as 'the craic'.

FOR THE FITZMAURICES OF GLENALAPPA

Nesta,
'Brood mare of the Geraldines',
Is where we began:

For six hundred years
Fitzmaurices, Fitzgeralds –
Nesta's clan,
Builders of abbeys
And castles,
Connoisseurs of poetry,
Horses and fine wine,
Were conquerors of the land.

But the Fitzmaurices,
Normans,
Had become 'more Irish than the Irish'
As time went on.

Our castles fell to Elizabeth,
The Lords of Kerry fell
(Except those who submitted
To England's will –
They kept their lands).

The builders of abbeys and castles
Are found in Kerry still
In small holdings
In glens like Glenalappa,
My ancestral home.
I travelled there this Christmas
With my son.

*

My father,
His father
And his father's father
Sat around the fire
At Christmas
In Glenalappa.

As I did.

The fire is out
This Christmas,
The house deserted,
No Fitzmaurice now
In Glenalappa.

Farewell
All the Toms, Dicks, Jacks,
Noras, Ellens, Margarets

In every generation
Who sat around the fire
In Glenalappa.

Where are you, this Christmas,
My people?

Everywhere but in Glenalappa.

And somewhere in New York,
First cousins I've never met,
Whose names I don't even know.

For all the fires that burned
At Christmas in Glenalappa,
For all the generations
Who sat around that fire,
For all my people,
Dead, alive or yet to be born
For whom this place is home,
Out of our history
I make this poem.

Fitzmaurice of Glenalappa.

ON FIRST MEETING THE MARQUESS OF LANSDOWNE

Listowel Castle, 21 April, 2005

The Marquess of Lansdowne is the direct descendant of Patrick Fitz-maurice, son of Thomas Fitzmaurice, eighteenth Lord Kerry. Patrick was five years old when Listowel castle, the last Fitzmaurice castle to hold out against Queen Elizabeth I, was besieged by Sir Charles Wilmot in November and December 1600. He was smuggled out of the castle upon its surrender. Patrick, nineteenth Lord Kerry, was captured, educated in England and raised in the Protestant faith.

'Which line do you belong to?' I don't know.
Too poor to trace, there's no record of my line.
Somewhere, somehow, long ago,
Someone, a Fitzmaurice, one of mine,
Left it all behind him and now I
Can't trace my line to castles. All I know
Is we left all that behind us, I don't know why
But know myself a poet, proudly low.
A rich man with a title finds his place
In history. It was ever so.
The rest of us are hard pressed to trace
Our great grandparents. It's enough to know
That, rooted in this place where I belong,
I turn our common history to song.

TRUE LOVE

They didn't sleep together in the end:
'True love', Mam called it from their double bed;
Her illness made her husband her best friend.
He took no other mate when she was dead.
They didn't sleep together in the end:
From mid-life on, my father slept alone;
I wonder how he felt being her best friend
But he didn't complain and stayed with her at home.
They didn't sleep together in the end:
There's more to love than self – they both knew this;
They loved enough to call each other 'friend' –
That's what it meant each night when they would kiss
Before Dad left their room to sleep alone.
True love it was. That's what kept them going.

HOMAGE TO THOMAS MacGREEVY

MacGreevy, poet, Catholic, you found your place
In a world where art redeemed, the word was true,
In a creed that raised living into grace
As, a poet and a Catholic, I must too.
The life a Catholic has to face
Is no different to the life we all go through
Losing heart at the squalid commonplace
But for a vision that redeems its ugly hue.
So welcome, then, the hopeless and the base,
The depths descended as their artists drew
Their Christs amid dejection and disgrace,
Christ my muse in poem, in pub, in pew.
With MacGreevy, poet, Catholic, I find my place
In a creed that raises living into grace.

A MIDDLE AGED ORPHEUS LOOKS BACK AT HIS LIFE

For Kris & Lisa Kristofferson

I took my voice to places where no man
Should take his voice and hope that it would sing.
All I wanted when I began
Was to strike up my guitar and do my thing.
Haunted from home, I sang my song
While all around forgot their words and fell;
In the underworld I blundered on
In regions where not it, but I, was hell.

I took my voice to places where no man
Should take his voice and hope that it would sing;
I paid the price in lines that rhyme and scan,
The last illusion to which singers cling
Before they yield their song up to the truth
They thought they could out-sing in foolish youth.

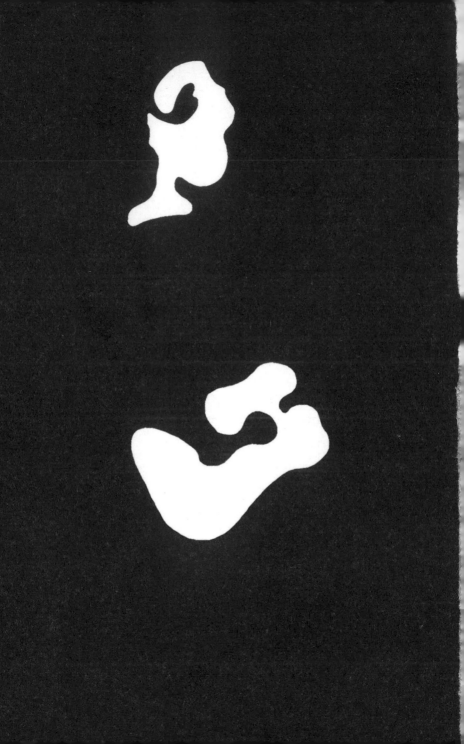